# FRENCH DRAWINGS

# GREAT DRAWINGS OF THE WORLD

# FRENCH DRAWINGS

From the 15th to the Early 19th Century

Text by Jean Vallery-Radot

SHOREWOOD PUBLISHERS INC. NEW YORK, N. Y.

Copyright © 1964 by Shorewood Publishers Inc.

All rights reserved

Library of Congress Catalog Card Number 64-22717

Printed by Shorewood Press, Plainview, N.Y.

# Contents

# FRENCH DRAWINGS

The drawing, by its intended goal as well as by the technique it uses and its resulting effects—this *unicum*—contrasts with engraving, which is obtained through etching and other means and multiplied by the printing press. But then, do not the one and the other stem from the same search for expressing form?

Though the drawing and the engraving appear in all periods of art history, both lacked a proper support to express themselves in usual practice. Such a support is paper, known in Europe as early as the Middle Ages, but the use of which became generalized only in the fifteenth century; this was the time when the printing press was invented—printed books calling for a large consumption of paper. This was also the time when the engraving, also printed on paper, took off on its flight—a flight more precocious than that of the drawing, for the latter, when executed with a metalpoint, required a paper prepared through a long and meticulous process.

But the draughtsmen needed a faster procedure. This was made available to them by the black stone, or Italian stone, which appeared in its homeland shortly before the end of the fifteenth century. The spread of its use on unprepared paper marks the advent of modern drawing. The mere ascertainment of this fact allows immediate evaluation of the importance of the various techniques with regard to the drawing—the pen, brush, metalpoint; the stones —black stone; sanguine, chalk, pastel, graphite (black lead). Some of these different techniques are very ancient—pen and brush; others, especially the stones, more recent. Graphite or lead pencil dates only from the nineteenth century.

All these means of expression were made available to the draughtsman. The artist's choice, increasingly free as the technical means multiplied, is revealing. The artistic temperament appears through the techniques thus selected, and through the tendencies thus expressed arise the styles. With their mutual, intimately mixed reactions, styles and techniques define the evolution, the milestones of which will be briefly recalled in the lines which follow.

Before the use of paper, drawing was usually done with a pen, either on parchment (sheepskin) or on vellum (calf-skin, finer than the former). This is how manuscript illuminations were drawn, but since their compositions are considered paintings, they are not classified as drawings—which are not often colored. However, the unfinished illuminations escape this discrimination for they reveal the lines, like the sinopia, or reddish-brown under-drawing, of an uncompleted fresco. One of the most extraordinary parts of Villard de Honnecourt's famous drawing album, from the middle of the thirteenth century, is devoted to "portraiture," which is a kind of image-drawing method. On geometrical canvases—generators of shapes—the author, with a pen both firm and flowing, inscribes decorative motives, animals, figures on foot or on horseback. His style is that of the stone-cutters of the contemporary cathedrals or churches, for which he sometimes also drew plans.

Sketching was also done with the brush. It is with the brush and India ink on white silk (tamit) that one of the masterpieces of the School of Paris, the so-called Parement de Narbonne altar-frontal, was executed (around 1375). It is sometimes compared to *An Archer* at Christ Church to which it apparently is closely related.

### XV CENTURY

The scarcity of preserved drawings, as well as their almost complete anonymity, gives only a vague idea about their evolution during that period. The attributions put forward by scholars are often subject to reconsideration.

The first years of the fifteenth century demonstrate that French drawing remained in the framework of the so-called international Gothic style. In the

Figure 1
Jacques CALLOT
*Portrait of Claude Deruet*
*and his son*
pen with washes of bistre
272 x 177 mm. (10 11/16 x 7")
Paris, Louvre   Inv. 25059

artistic milieu of Paris in the time of Charles VI (1380-1442), where the contributions from the Netherlands and Italy merged, it is difficult to sort out the strictly French elements. Such is the problem set up about most of the drawings of that period, of which those presented at the exhibition in 1957, in the Drawing Room of The Louvre showed excellent examples: *Death, Assumption and Coronation of the Blessed Virgin,* and *Saint Jerome,* rightly compared to that of the frontispiece of the *Illuminated Bible* (historical) by Pol de Limburg (around 1410); graceful scenes recalling the courteous and knightly life, daintily drawn on vellum, one with a metalpoint, the other with a wonderfully delicate pen; precious techniques in perfect harmony with the elegant gentility of the figures represented—*Young Girl Holding a Hawk,* the *Young Falconer between Two Noble Ladies.*

In powerful contrast with this rather fragile aristocratic art, the Master of the so-called Hours of Rohan expresses his emotion at the sight of suffering and death with a dramatic intensity. The paralytic of the *Bathing-pool of Bethesda* (around 1418), is really the brother of the *Dead Man Before His Judge.* This dead man—with a voice from beyond—opens a pathetic dialogue with God.

The other great master is Jean Fouquet, whose portrait of Guillaume Juvenal des Ursins, a study for the painting of 1460, marks a turning-point in the history of French drawing. This drawing on paper, done with black stone and colored pencils, is indeed the most ancient in this technique in France recorded to date. At the same time, it is the marvellous achievement of a portrait in powerful relief, reflecting the calm self-confidence of the model, with a feeling of wide human understanding. It is the beginning of modern drawing in French art. Its author brought illumination to such a perfection that one can say, with M. Jean Porcher, that the history of this art finished with him. Fouquet, thus, was both a beginning and an end.

To those two great artists must be added two others: René d'Anjou, King of Sicily (1408-1480), and the Master of Moulins. The first one, son of Louis II of Anjou, was familiarly called "René the Good." The Print-Room of the

Paris Bibliothèque Nationale keeps his beautiful portrait, drawn with pen, on paper, and water-colored. He was not only a great patron of art—a Maecenas —but also an artist whose fame has been in eclipse. Recent research has attracted attention to the famous *Book of the Love-smitten Heart,* in the Vienna National Library, of which he was the admirable designer. His water-color drawings were equally remarkable, and illustrate two specimens of the *Book of Tourneys,* preserved at the Paris Bibliothèque Nationale.

Jacques Dupont has credited the *Profile of a Young Woman* (around 1480) to the Master of Moulins. This magnificent pen-drawing on paper was acquired recently by The Louvre. Another drawing, *Young Girl Seated,* also in the Louvre, previously credited to the same master, has not been unanimously accepted.

At the turn of the century, which was to become the century of the French Renaissance, a new feeling was developing in Jean Colombe, one of the last illuminators, heir to Fouquet, and whom we mention here for his uncompleted paintings of the *History of the Destruction of Troy* (around 1500). In these impetuous pen drawings, which prove the mastery of his hand, his already mannered taste characterized one of the aspects of the close of the Middle Ages. It was the symptom of a general tendency which the Italian masters shortly expressed and transmitted to the School of Fontainebleau, as well as to the whole of Europe of that time.

### XVI CENTURY

The sixteenth century was, in France, the century of Renaissance, an event of first importance, which gave the arts and humanities a new and lasting orientation. But in comparison with that of the Italian Quattrocento, the French Renaissance was a belated one. This chronological lag had important consequences.

Since the High Renaissance, art had largely evolved in Italy. It was introduced in France at various moments of its evolution, which were manifold transformations of its primary spirit. Thus, for example, the first decorative elements which appeared in the French chateaux of still purely Gothic structure, were borrowed from North Italy's edifices, where an abundance of decoration prevailed over the principles of classic composition. The School of Fontainebleau's beginnings date from another, more advanced, time of this evolution, as will be seen farther on.

It is rather with difficulty that one follows the evolution of French drawing during the sixteenth century, because of the relatively few works preserved to our day. This scarcity is due to multiple causes. Above all, two reasons must be kept in mind, as shown in Jean Adhémar's excellent book *French Drawings of the XVI Century:* on one hand, the natural destruction and disappearance of drawings in the course of the centuries; on the other hand, their attribution to other masters. Undoubtedly some collections and albums have been preserved, but they concern only the artist or artists whose works have been gathered into such groups.

Therefore, instead of a general knowledge of this evolution, one must be satisfied with partial surveys, which are like chapters extracted from an incomplete book. Among these surveys, however, two major tendencies, considered characteristically French, stand out in full light. One concerns pencil-drawn portraits, the other the School of Fontainebleau.

The portraits drawn with crayons (pencils), which came into such high favor during the sixteenth century, had had precedents. Fouquet's portrait of Guillaume Juvenal des Ursins, already mentioned, must not have been an isolated example. But the elegant and sumptuous court life under the later Valois rulers created an exceptionally favorable milieu for their expansion. Their extraordinary vogue started with Jean Clouet.

Of Flemish origin, this artist worked at the French court, where the royal account-books indicate his presence in 1516. He died around 1541. His drawings, of which the Condé Museum in Chantilly has an important collection, were acquired by the Duc d'Aumale, in 1890. They are broadly treated with black stone, often heightened with sanguine, as the one of Odet de Foix, Lord of Lautrec. The artist concentrates his attention on the faces and disregards

Figure 2
Pierre MIGNARD · *James II and His Family* · black chalk, heightened with white, on gray paper,
230 x 320 mm. (9 x 12⅝") · Paris, Louvre

the rest. He scans the physiognomy and, through its features, discovers at the same time the psychology of the person represented. The relief, which gives the face all its depth, is obtained very simply in the shadings, through parallel hachures, drawn diagonally, and with the white of the paper retaining the highlights. Thus, by extremely economical means, the artist obtains maximum effects. Their classic simplicity makes one think of certain Italian influences. His unadorned art, which impresses by its nobleness, makes him one of the greatest draughtsmen of the French Renaissance.

At the time of Jean Clouet, the engraver Jean Duvet (who had a strong personality) and Jean Cousin the Elder, native of Sens, were also working. Where are the drawings of Jean Duvet, beside the *Father Eternal* in The Louvre, attributed to him by P. Lavallée? Those of Jean Cousin remain subjects of discussion. The drawings of the engraver Jean de Gourmont, whose activity was centered in Lyon, under the pretense of studies of perspective, actually depict New Testament scenes *(Massacre of the Innocents, Christ at the Pillar)* in columned palaces.

François I had been able to persuade Leonardo da Vinci to come from Italy and settle near Amboise, in 1517, but the great master was to die two years later. When this same king invited Rosso to Fontainebleau, in 1530, and Primaticcio, in 1532, the evolution of art in Italy had accelerated. Therefore, it was a new, more advanced stage of this evolution represented by the two Italian painters destined to exert such a deep influence on French art. This stage of development took place about ten years after Raphael's death. The principles, which the painter of the Vatican Stanzas brought to triumph in his classic compositions, had already been shaken. The great art of the High Renaissance was fading. Rosso and Primaticcio, creators of the School of Fontainebleau and introducers of Mannerism into France, were heirs to a great tradition which had already deteriorated.

At the Chateau of Fontainebleau, in the François I Gallery, Rosso framed his painted compositions in a stucco ornamentation, mingling large nude figures with garlands of fruits and scrolls, imitating cut-out leather. The engravings, executed according to these new decorations, have spread widely the fame of the School of Fontainebleau's style. Few of Rosso's drawings are known but enough, nevertheless, to note the different feeling which enlivens those made before his departure for France *(Virgin of Mercy)*, and those made after his arrival in Fontainebleau. The later drawings, according to P. Du Colombier, are rough and angular with contempt for versimilitude—their anatomy more asserted than exact, their hard-featured faces grimacing with an excess of expression—and deserve a popularity they have never received. This quotation describes well Rosso's drawing of *Vertumnus and Pomona* (The Louvre), done for the destroyed "Cabinet de Pomone" in Fontainebleau.

The appearance of this new viewpoint accounts for the fact that the Italian master, on his way from Venice to Paris, went through Switzerland, where he had a revelation of Germanic art. This is explained in Mr. Adhémar's excellent book *French Drawings in the XVI Century*. Rosso died in 1540; Jean Clouet shortly thereafter. The former was replaced by Primaticcio who, henceforth, except for a slight interruption, was going to be the sole master of Fontainebleau's works. François Clouet succeeded his father in the functions of Painter for the King. Considering them as draughtsmen, both are very different from those they had replaced.

To the hard and incisive line of Rosso, contrast the softly-curved contours in which Primaticcio wrapped his figures. He followed at first the manner of Jules Romain, whose pupil he had been, before being inspired by the manner of Parmigianino, whom he knew only through drawings. Thereafter, the elongated legs, the longer slender neck, the smaller head determined the proportions of this new canon of beauty, well-demonstrated by one of his pen-and-wash drawings preserved in The Louvre. This study for one of the stucco frames of the Duchesse d'Estampes's room at Fontainebleau sets off the harmonious and flexible line of the nudes conceived following his new esthetic principles. It was in this style that he drew from then on, and that he decorated the Henry II Gallery, as well as the huge Ulysses' Gallery (later destroyed), assisted by Niccolo Dell'Abbate, whose drawing we point out in passing. This style inspired many subsequent artists.

Among numerous drawings linked with the School of Fontainebleau style, we recall *Games of Childhood* and *Music,* by the engraver Etienne Delaune, whose albums of decorative models were engraved with chiseller's precision, and those by Antoine Caron, who enhanced Mannerism even more than did the Fontainebleau style, as observed in his compositions of the *Artemis Suite,* preserved in the Print Room of the Bibliothèque Nationale.

François Clouet, who succeeded his father in 1541, attained success very rapidly. Portrait painter of kings, he also painted princes, courtiers and noble ladies. Held in high esteem by Catherine de' Medici, people fought for his "crayons" (sketches), which vogue he brought to its peak. His father's talent was revived in them, but with less fullness. P. Lavallée wrote: "His art is less vigorous; the artist has an extremely delicate and keen eye, although he remains the slave of the line." The father's portraits are human documents; those of the son are marvellous iconographic documents, but without the same depth.

François Clouet was to have emulators, among whom—the Dumonstiers, Etienne and Pierre I; and soon after, numerous followers, such as Benjamin Foulon and François Quesnel, who do not compare with the predecessors. The fashion for crayon-drawn portraits was not going to fade. At the end of the century, the best representative of this long tradition was Master I.D.C., whose lovely portrait of Gabrielle d'Estrées, Henri IV's mistress, one admires.

The activity of the Second School of Fontainebleau, which had no link with the first, was to be carried on into the next century, but only for a short while.

The XVII century was to inherit a style, "Mannerism," destined to disappear rapidly, and a genre, that of the "crayons" (drawn portraits), the vogue of which was only to end with Louis XIII's reign. Other inheritances, more lasting, were landscape and architectural drawing which Etienne Dupérac and Jacques Androuet Du Cerceau were to transmit to the next century.

Figure 3
Jean-Antoine GROS
*Page from a Sketchbook:*
*Horses and Sappho*
pen and bistre wash
230 x 165 mm. (9 x 6½")
Paris, Louvre

Figure 4
*Page from a Sketchbook:*
*Studies of Horses*
pen and bistre wash
230 x 165 mm. (9 x 6½")
Paris, Louvre

## XVII CENTURY

The title given by Voltaire to his well-known work, *The Century of Louis XIV*, gave support for a long time to the fiction of the unity of the Grand Siècle, which, on the contrary, had manifold aspects. It has been realized for a long time that the seventeenth was not merely the century of Louis XIV, the young monarch having only begun to reign by himself in 1661. Inseparable from the change in ideas and the literary evolution, multiple artistic tendencies blossomed in the course of that secular era. Master drawings were the "first thoughts" of these trends.

At the beginning of the century, Mannerism was prolonged only to underscore its passing with the Second School of Fontainebleau, represented by Ambroise Dubois, Toussaint Dubreuil and Martin Fréminet. On the other hand, Mannerism was still glittering with dazzling but ephemeral glamor, in the artistic milieu of Nancy, enlivened by the festivities of the brilliant court of the Dukes of Lorraine.

The figures in Bellange's compositions have an ambiguous charm and slender forms. Clothed with either puffed-out or clinging materials, they were the ultimate descendants of the long Mannerist style, the elegant and graceful end of a period which swaggered in affected poses. Skillful in the handling of fluid wash-drawing in mellow tints, Bellange also made use, with even more talent, of a supple sanguine which, a century later, was to be used by Jean Antoine Watteau.

Next to Mannerism, whose days were numbered, Realism, another course of an antipodal tendency, existed. Even Bellange had occasionally made concessions to this trend in his etchings. And Lagneau, in his portraits, expressed it often, with a caricatural purpose, in the early years of the century.

The most famous of the French engravers of Realism, and at the same time one of the greatest draughtsmen of the century, Callot, born in the Mannerist milieu of Nancy, met other Mannerists, first in Rome, then in Florence. But, very early, Callot turned away from them, drawing his inspiration from everyday life, scrutinizing the people he came across with a piercing eye, at festivities and fairs, in the city and the country. He outlined, in quick and wonderful sketches, their faces, gestures, attitudes and even the motion which animated them; sketches of the most infallible hand at the service of the most trained eye. This is what his drawings, done with pen only, show—like the horse serial from *Tempesta*—as well as those with sanguine—like the sketches for the *Impruneta*—or those with pen-and-bistre washes, of which he made painterly use as a creator of space and light.

The Baroque Rome of Urban VIII was hospitable to French painters. Working in the environment of masters trained in the studio of Annibale Carracci, they also remembered Caravaggio. When they were on their way back to France, they seldom failed to go through Venice, which instilled in them new inspirations.

These returning artists, each one affected in a different manner, were, following Charles Sterling's term, "as many French renderings of the Baroque art." The return, in 1627, of Simon Vouet, who soon after became the chief of a famous studio, was an event. His sketches, drawn with black stone on fawn-colored paper, are as vigorous as his models were sturdy. They were popular types of Caravaggio's lineage which one finds again in the painter's compositions. Similarly, there were also Claude Vignon who returned, adorning his models with plumes; François Pérrier, author of a black-stone drawing *Time Cutting the Wings of Love,* which he engraved himself; Sébastien Bourdon, whose *Crucifixion of Saint Peter,* one of his studies for a "May" in Notre Dame, was appreciated by Mariette; Pierre Blanchard, who, according to Dezallier d'Argenville, "had a particular talent for painting half-bodied Virgins" and whose too scanty drawings are probably preparatory studies.

The Baroque influence of which all these drawings give evidence is one of the main aspects of French art during the reign of Louis XIII. The diversity of French art during that period is remarkable and presents other aspects. But in the frame itself of this Baroque civilization, signs soon foretell another esthetic trend. This one is no longer founded on imagination, but on thought, no longer founded on abundance of setting or of style, but on restraint and subordination of the details to the whole, no longer founded on the effect, but on the expression—all principles which were to triumph in classic art.

Poussin was still a Mannerist when he left Paris in 1624. In Rome, where he had been fully aware of the contemporary artistic streams, he rapidly mastered these influences, drew conclusions from his elaborate studies of antique art, and became the chief of the classical school. The evolution of style in his drawings illustrates this in a striking manner. At the beginning, it is the draughtsman who predominates. A gray wash lightly shades the emphasized outlines of the drawings for the poem *Adonis* by Marino; then, very soon, the painter prevails. The accents of the bistre wash give more and more relief to the composition. Upon Poussin's return to Rome after a brief stay in Paris, his style became noble and austere, with powerful contrasts of shade and highlight. Then, as he grew old, his hand no longer obeyed him. The simplified drawings, with shapes of the master's old age, are recognized by their shaky line, traced out by his unsteady hand. His *Study of Trees at Daybreak* (The Louvre) in pen-and-bistre wash is one of those "beautiful accidents of light," of which Félibien spoke in connection with his landscape drawings, which, like those of Claude Lorrain, express a feeling for nature unique at the time and which reappear only in the nineteenth century.

Claude Lorrain had returned to Rome and settled there in 1627. Elsheimer had died there in 1610 but his memory still lived. Claude Lorrain did not ignore anything concerning his "arcadies" and their chiaroscuro, but, above everything else, nature had been his great educator. His friend Joachim Sandrart described him as wholly engrossed by his studies in the open air, spending entire days in the Roman country from dawn to twilight, sensitive to the effects of light at all hours, but especially to sunrise and sunset, and attentive to the study of distances. For having marked them down in a few strokes of the pen, enhanced with touches of bistre wash of a marvellous sensitivity, Claude Lorrain became ranked among the greatest masters of the pen-and-brush drawing.

To the classical esthetic art defined by Poussin, correspond Philippe de

Figure 5
Jean-Auguste-Dominique INGRES
*Preliminary Study for the Portrait
of Comtesse d'Haussonville*
graphite and black crayon
369 x 189 mm. (14½ x 7 7/16")
New York, The Frick Collection

25

Champaigne's portraits of a Jansenistical austerity, of which too few drawings exist; Le Sueur's sketches for his decoration of the Chartreux's Cloister and of the Muses' Room in the Hotel Lambert in Paris; the sculptor Sarrazin's scanty drawings, among which, in particular, is the black-stone *Mascaron* in the Stockholm National Museum.

The great classical art of Poussin, once it became reduced to a formula, is, in short, the definition of Academism. It is the price of guided art, which reached its climax under the artistic dictatorship of Le Brun (1664-1683), director of the Academy and great craftsman of Louis XIV's official style. But Le Brun, successively a pupil of Perrier and Vouet, had previously sojourned in Rome and remembered his various training. His academic art, therefore, represents not only a unique aspect of this complex painter, whose best drawings, paradoxically, are those which deviate from Academism. Apart from Academism, some artists worked in complete independence. Preceded by Mellan, who had brought back from Rome the fashion of the small "Italian style" portrait, in black stone and sanguine, Nanteuil drew and engraved purely classical "character portraits." In his landscape drawings, as well as in his paintings, Van der Meulen gave a great lesson of Flemish sincerity. Raymond de La Fage, who worked in Rome, presented himself as a fine, free bacchanalian artist. Jacques Courtois, known as "the Burgundian," worked also in Rome. His pen-and-bistre-wash drawings show the same fire as his battle paintings. Pierre Puget's Baroque art expressed itself powerfully in his all-too-rare drawings.

Around 1680, the crisis of European conscience was awakening. It brought everything in question, pointing to an orientation which was to be that of the eighteenth century. The philosophy, of which Locke laid down the principles in 1690, was based on reason. Already the forerunners of the art of the eighteenth century were appearing. The victory of the Rubenists over the Poussinists was one of color over drawing. As far back as 1680, a pupil of Le Brun, Charles de La Fosse, had inaugurated at the Academy a teaching policy of emphasizing color in categorical opposition with the linear principles previously professed in that institution. His three-pencils (*trois-crayons*) technique was one which Watteau was to adopt with success.

A new spirit enlivened the artists' inspiration. The "Grand Manner" was out of date. From the majestic one glided into the graceful. With Antoine Coypel, virtuoso of the three-pencils technique and one of the chief originators of the change of style at the frontier of the two centuries, the divinities of Olympus became familiar. His *Venus on the Waters,* which is seen in a charming trois-crayons drawing on gray paper, is nothing more than a pretty swimmer. It looks as if, once the parenthesis on the classical time closed, Callot's art was reviving in the drawings of Sébastien Le Clerc and of Gillot, who became Watteau's master. Paving the way for the *fêtes galantes,* Bernard Picart, on a charming sanguine drawing preserved in the Ashmolean Museum, represented couples sitting in shady places in a park.

Thus, little by little, all the elements of a renewed art were gathering. Merely genius was missing to carry them out. Genius was to be Watteau's role. With him, the curtain rises on the eighteenth-century art.

### XVIII CENTURY AND BEGINNING OF THE XIX CENTURY

Watteau's art prevailed over the first half of the eighteenth century, and its radiant influence was to be felt until the Davidian reaction near the end of the century. With Watteau, painting had again become sensitive to the charms of color and light. He also introduced color and light into drawing. At first, he sketched with black stone and sanguine. Next, he developed a new technique, after having had the opportunity to admire and study the drawings of the great amateur Crozat's famous collection. He even copied a few of them and was especially interested by those of the great Venetians and the Flemish, among others Rubens, of whom he already knew the paintings in the Medici Gallery in the Luxemburg. Educated through the lessons of these great colorists, he added the chalk for brilliant highlights to the sanguine and the black stone. Henceforth, it is the *trois-crayons* technique which was his—like Rubens'. From here on began the great Watteau period, his "good days", as

Gersaint said. Who could describe the mastery and at the same time the un-equalled charm of these sheets of paper, covered with studies, drawn in the presence of the model, without particular goal; the vigorous and fine elegance of these figures, caught in their attitudes and expressions? Watteau would choose a few of these studies whenever he fancied, gathering them on canvas, under shady places in a park of dreams.

In Watteau's wake followed Lancret, Pater and Portail. All the genre are represented among the artists of that period, who were, at the same time, craftsmen. There were great portraitists like the pastelist La Tour, whose "preparations" are all deep psychological studies; vignette-engravers, like Cochin, Eisen, Gravelot; landscapists and animalists, like J. B. Oudry, and so on. But one must put the great painter Chardin on a pedestal. He painted still life, portraits, and scenes of bourgeois indoor life. Only a few drawings by him are known; among them, *The Bowler,* which impresses by its broad and powerful technique.

The art of the French Regency, which Watteau incarnates, was succeeded by the Rococo style, which Boucher, a born decorator, represents perfectly in all manners of approach. "Its prettiness is the soul of time and Boucher's genius." This nineteenth-century appreciation by the de Goncourt brothers not only precisely describes Boucher's art, but also fixes its limits. The numer-ous nudes which he drew with mastery give excellent proof of his "genius of prettiness."

Fragonard's sanguines would have been sufficient to classify him as the greatest draughtsman of the second half of the century. Compared to him, his friend Hubert Robert was outshone. Later, Fragonard was attracted by another means of expression—wash drawing. With this technique he was more painter than draughtsman, and still surpassed himself by obtaining effects of Rembrandtesque chiaroscuro of an exceptional mastery.

The witty, sometimes flippant art of Fragonard was the exact opposite of Greuze, who moralized in painting. But, when confronted with reality, he reacted with happy sincerity. His sanguine drawings are as vigorously con-

Figure 6

Théodore Géricault • *Study for the Raft of the Medusa—The Ship Sighted* • pen and ink,
200 x 280 mm. (7⅞ x 11") • Rouen, Musée des Beaux-Arts

29

structed as his painted portraits, as well as his wash drawings touched with pen strokes.

Among the numerous Little Masters, Gabriel de Saint-Aubin, painter, draughtsman and engraver, deserves a separate place. He had first aspired to be a historical painter, that is to say, of "lofty" subjects. His failure brought him a witty consolation, a poem by his friend Sedaine, which at the same time was excellent advice:

> Leave all these Homeric heroes alone,...
> ...Sketch rather for Cythera
> On some tender and gallant subject.
> A trifle, a light drawing
> On this square of white paper.

Those "trifles," those "light drawings," made the renown of Saint-Aubin, the greatest of the minor artists of the period of Louis XV. He was, through his delightfully-quick sketches, unequalled as chronicler of this age.

At that time, the draughtsman-engraver also attracted attention. They used, indifferently, one or the other technique, with dazzling virtuosity in each. But is this virtuosity itself not a stumbling block? One could admire, without restraint, the drawings of the most famous among them, Moreau le Jeune, if precisely they were not too polished, too "well done."

In the eighteenth century, there was a turning point of taste about 1750. It is at this time that the impulse of a "return to antiquity," initiated by the theorists and the critics, became dominant. However, this trend had to overcome opposition, and was to triumph with David barely a few years before the French Revolution.

Neo-Classicism stemmed from the "return to antiquity." David's *Oath of the Horatii,* triumphantly welcomed at the Paris Salon in 1785, was the official manifesto and marked the advent of the style. The exclusive worship of the antique thus established a rigid and cold style which put heroes with

Spartan virtues on a pedestal. The new style clashed violently with the brilliant, elegant, pleasant, often dissolute art, which had reigned until then but was condemned in advance by the new esthetics and blown away by the revolutionary turmoil at the same time as the society of the Ancien Régime, of which it had been a reflection.

David, the leader of the new academy, took the chance of inscribing what one could call the "attitude" of a crowd in motion, in his sketches for *The Oath of the Tennis Court.* In his individual sketches for Napoleon's coronation, he studied in detail the physiognomies of the figures, leaving striking portraits of the pope, Pius VII, and of Napoleon crowning himself.

At the junction of the eighteenth and nineteenth centuries, Prud'hon's art recalled a nostalgic remembrance of the past and opened a new outlook to the future. He borrowed figures and allegories from antiquity, but they appear to be wrapped in a Correggian softness. His work is redolent of the love of Greece. As in the century in which he was born, Prud'hon still used black stone and chalk to make the lights glitter, thus bringing out a richness of rounded and supple forms others rarely equalled. This was his instinctive reaction against the primacy of line, the fundamental dogma of the Neo-Classical school. No one followed the dogma with a more inflexible rigor than Ingres, its most convinced and fervent admirer. In the midst of the French Revolution, Conté put the finishing touches to the manufacture of the graphite pencil, called a lead-pencil. In it Ingres found the most fitting technique for his ideal. With an apparently unperturbed sensitivity, he got from this technique, in his own words, everything one can ask from a drawing: "expression, structure, form, draft, relief." The portraits executed before and during his sojourn in Rome (1806-1824) are all masterpieces.

Neoclassical art had the coldness of the marble statues which inspired it. Soon, an urge for escape, a return to life, color and motion awakened. In an impetuous fieriness, Gros' drawings expressed this feeling, a dramatic contradiction between his own temperament and his fidelity to the Davidian discipline, and which explains the reasons for his suicide.

Géricault reconciled the contraries—antiquity and present time—in opening the road to the future. He followed passionately, although coldbloodedly, his studies of the antique. It was in carrying over to contemporary life the sum of these studies that Géricault instilled a powerful life to his figures, caught in full action. They have the bulkiness and the compactness of the sculptural shapes with which his visual memory was filled. His drawings are intimate witnesses to his ardent search. *The Carabinier Officer* is an equestrian statue, a living statue, carried into the gallop of a charge, man and mount bursting forth with a vigor which is already expending itself.

Géricault died in 1824, the very year Delacroix presented *The Massacre at Chios* at the Paris Salon. The Romantic School was beginning.

JEAN VALLERY-RADOT

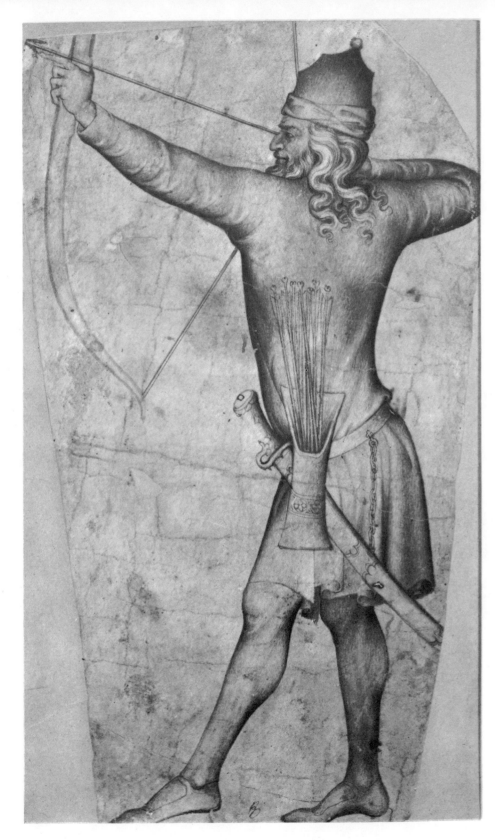

Plate 1
Master of the PAREMENT
of Narbonne
*An Archer*
brush and black ink on vellum
(cut irregularly at sides), 267 x 160 mm.
(10½ x 6⁵⁄₁₆″)
Oxford, Christ Church

Plate 2

ANONYMOUS French Master · *Three Ladies* · pen drawing with light India ink wash outlining the forms, on parchment prepared with white, the faces heightened with vermillion, 104 x 186 mm. (4⅛ x 7⁵⁄₁₆″) · Paris, Louvre

Plate 3
FRENCH · *Three Studies of a Madonna and Child* · silverpoint on green prepared paper, heightened in white, 115 x 209 mm. (4½ x 8¼") · Basel, Kupferstichkabinett

36

Plate 4
Jean FOUQUET
*Study for the Portrait of*
*Guillaume Juvenal des Ursins*
black and colored chalks on
prepared paper, 266 x 195 mm.
(10½ x 7 ¹¹⁄₁₆″)
Berlin, Kupferstichkabinett

Plate 5
ANONYMOUS French
*Standing Ecclesiastic with*
*Folded Hands*
pen and black ink, body-color in red
and brown, heightened with white
on gray-colored paper
280 x 125 mm. (11 x 4¹⁵⁄₁₆″)
Rotterdam, Museum Boymans-van
Beuningen

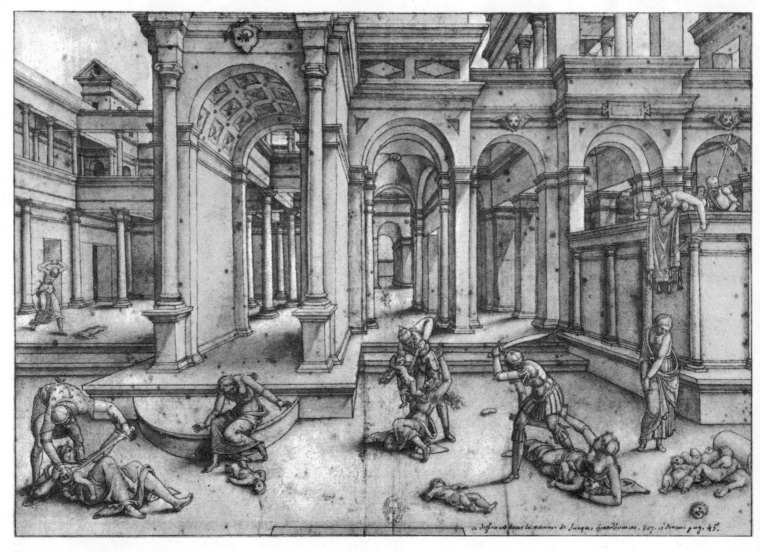

Plate 6

Jean de GOURMONT · *Massacre of the Innocents* · pen and wash on white paper, 210 x 320 mm. (8¼ x 12⅝")
Paris, Bibliothèque Nationale

Plate 7
School of FOUNTAINBLEAU • *Diana Hunting* • pen and bistre wash, heightened with white on tinted paper (2 sheets joined)
387 x 553 mm. (15¼ x 9¾") • Rennes, Musée des Beaux-Arts

La Balliue de Cam

Plate 8
Jean CLOUET
*The Widow of the
Bailiff of Caen*
red and black chalk
276 x 190 mm. (10⅞ x 7½")
Chantilly, Musée Condé

Plate 9
Jean CLOUET
*Odet de Foix, Seigneur de
Lautrec* (detail)
black and red chalk with traces
of water color at bottom
255 x 185 mm. (10¹⁄₁₆ x 7⁵⁄₁₆")
Chantilly, Musée Condé

_e $\mathcal{S}^r$ de lescu

41

Pierre belange.

Plate 11
Jacques CALLOT • *Sketches of Ballet Dancers* • red crayon on white paper, 210 x 287 mm. (8¼ x 11⁵⁄₁₆") • Art Institute of Chicago
Gift of the Print and Drawing Club

Plate 10
Jacques BELLANGE • *The Three Marys at the Tomb* • red chalk on white paper, 219 x 173 mm.
(8⅝ x 6¹³⁄₁₆") • Vienna, Albertina Gallery

Plate 12
François CLOUET
*René de la Jaille* (detail)
black and red chalk on
ivory paper, 292 x 205 mm.
(11½ x 8⅟₁₆")
Cambridge, Massachusetts
Harvard University
Courtesy of the
Fogg Art Museum

Plate 13
Master I.D.C.
*Gabrielle d'Estrées*
(Duchesse de Beaufort)
(detail)
black and red chalk on
white paper, 351 x 249 mm.
(13¹³⁄₁₆ x 9¹³⁄₁₆")
Paris, Bibliothèque Nationale

46

Plate 16
CLAUDE Lorrain · *Trees* · pen and bistre wash on blue paper, 200 x 260 mm. (7⅞ x 10¼") · New York, The Lehman Collection

Plate 17
François LAGNEAU
*Head of an Old Woman*
red and black crayon
the background tinted with
gray-green water color
298 x 228 mm. (11¾ x 9")
New York, John S. Newberry

49

Plate 18

Nicolas POUSSIN · *Moses Striking Water from the Rock* · black chalk and bistre wash, heightened with white, 170 x 255 mm.
(6 11/16 x 10 1/16") · Paris, Louvre

Plate 19

Nicolas POUSSIN · *Study for Rape of the Sabines* · pen and bistre wash, 164 x 219 mm. (6⁷⁄₁₆ x 8⅝")
Devonshire Collection, Chatsworth. Reproduced by Permission of the Trustees of the Chatsworth Settlement.

Plate 21
CLAUDE Lorrain
*Trees and Vines*
pen and bistre wash on blue paper
275 x 210 mm. (10¹³⁄₁₆ x 8¼")
Bayonne, Musée Bonnat

Plate 20
Robert NANTEUIL · *Marin Cureau de la Chambre, Physician to the King*
pencil on vellum, 140 x 98 mm. (5½ x 3⅞") · Washington, D.C.
National Gallery, Rosenwald Collection

53

Nicolas POUSSIN · *The Triumph of Bacchus* · pen and bistre, 157 x 228 mm. (6³⁄₁₆ x 9″) · Kansas City, Missouri,
Nelson Gallery of Art

Plate 23

Nicolas POUSSIN • *Judgment of Solomon* • pen and bistre wash over black chalk, 248 x 384 mm. (9¾ x 15⅛")
Paris, École Nationale Supérieure des Beaux-Arts

Plate 24
Jean BERAIN
*Costume Study for a
Carrousel (or Tournament),
No. I* • pen with India ink
and bistre wash
395 x 590 mm.
(15½ x 23¼")
Paris
Musée des Arts Decoratifs

Plate 25
Jean BERAIN
*Costume Study for a
Carrousel (or Tournament),
No. II* · pen with India ink
and bistre wash
395 x 590 mm.
(15½ x 23¼")
Paris
Musée des Arts Decoratifs

57

Plate 26

CLAUDE Lorrain • *Two Deer* • black chalk and bistre wash, 152 x 126 mm. (6 x 4¹⁵⁄₁₆")
Bradford, Pennsylvania, T. Edward Hanley

Plate 27
CLAUDE Lorrain
*Campagna Landscape*
pen, bistre and wash
320 x 215 mm.
(12⅝ x 8½")
London, The British Museum

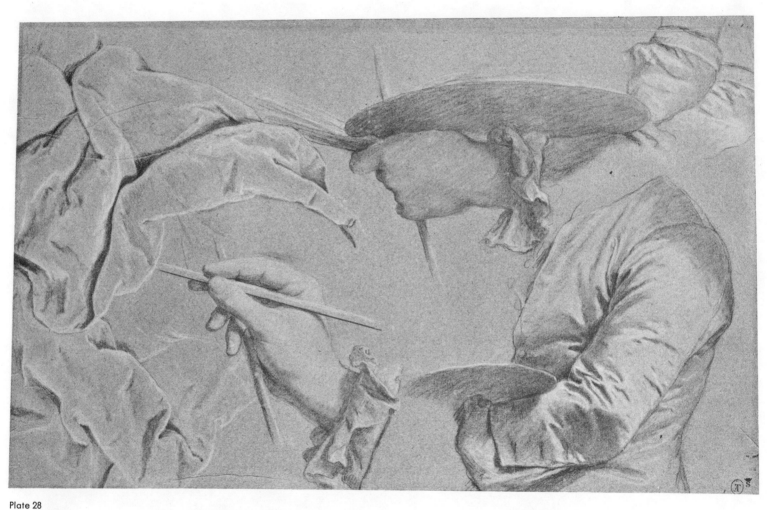

Plate 28
Hyacinth RIGAUD • *Partial Studies for his Self-Portrait at the Easel* • black and white chalk on blue paper, 284 x 458 mm.
(11³⁄₁₆ x 18¹⁄₁₆") • Cologne, Wallraf-Richartz Museum

Plate 29
Jean Antoine WATTEAU
*Three Studies of the Head
of a Young Negro* (detail)
black chalk, two shades of red chalk
with white wash and gray-green
water color, on cream paper, 243 x 271 mm.
(9⁹⁄₁₆ x 10¹¹⁄₁₆") • Paris, Louvre

60

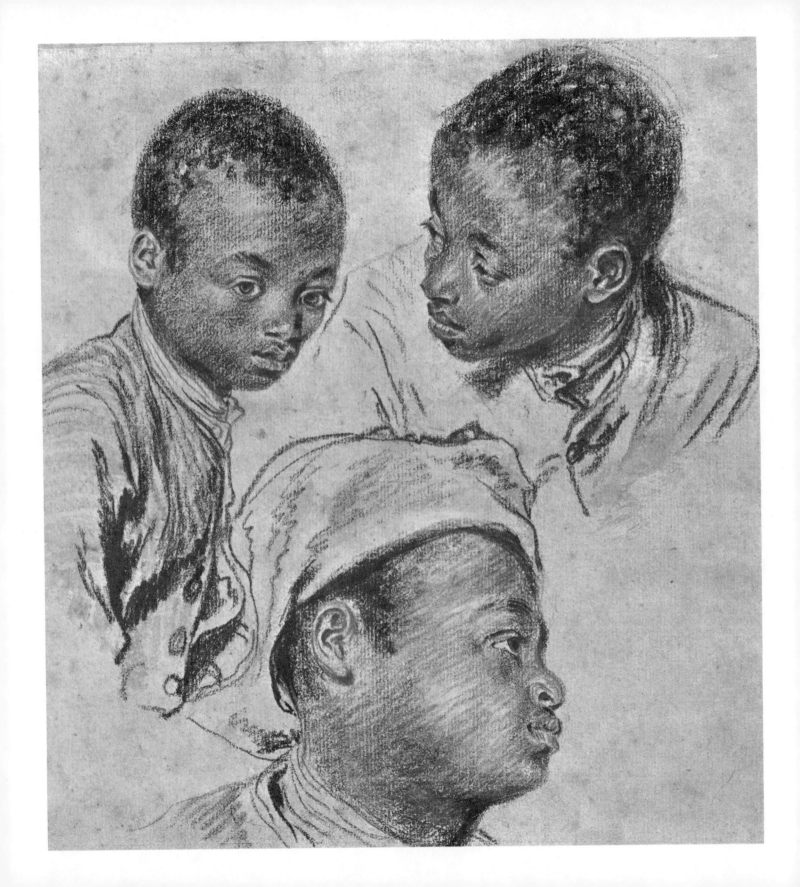

**Plate 30**

Eustache LE SUEUR • *Three Studies of a Carthusian* • black and white chalk on tan paper, 419 x 254 mm. (10 x 16½")
Rhode Island, Private Collection

Plate 31
Eustache LE SUEUR
*The Muse Erato*
black chalk, heightened with white
on gray paper, 380 x 240 mm.
(14¹⁵⁄₁₆ x 9⁷⁄₁₆") • Paris
École Nationale Supérieure
des Beaux-Arts

Plate 32

Jean Antoine WATTEAU • *Study for "La Famille"* • red, black and white chalk on gray-yellow paper, 325 x 330 mm. (12¹³⁄₁₆ x 13")
New York, Mrs. I. Straus

Plate 33
Jean Antoine WATTEAU
*Woman Seen at Half-Length* (detail)
red, black and white chalk on
yellowed cream paper, 249 x 184 mm.
(9¹³⁄₁₆ x 7¼") • Paris, Louvre

65

**Plate 34**

Israel SILVESTRE • *Villa Ludovisi* • pencil, brownish-yellow and green wash, 203 x 315 mm. (8 x 12⅜") • Cambridge, Massachusetts
Harvard University, Courtesy of the Fogg Art Museum

Plate 35
André Charles BOULLE
*Designs for torchere and a
chest of drawers*
pen with sepia and India ink
wash over red crayon, 630 x 355 mm.
(24¾ x 14")
Paris, Musée des Arts Decoratifs

Plate 36
Jean-Baptiste-Siméon CHARDIN
*Portrait of Françoise-
Marguerite Pouget*
pastel, 458 x 380 mm. (18 x 15")
Art Institute of Chicago
Joseph and Helen Regenstein
Collection

Plate 37
Jean Antoine WATTEAU
*Man Standing*
black, red and white chalk
on gray-brown paper
271 x 189 mm. (10¹¹⁄₁₆ x 7⁷⁄₁₆")
Rotterdam
Museum Boymans-van Beuningen

Plate 38

Alexander François DESPORTES · *Tiger* · black, red and white crayon on tan paper, 395 x 570 mm. (15½ x 22½") · Paris, Louvre

Plate 39
Claude GILLOT
*Two Actors*
red chalk on cream paper
200 x 159 mm. (7⅞ x 6¼")
New York, Mrs. H. A. Metzger

70

71

**Plate 40**

Jean-Baptiste OUDRY · *Still Life with Parrot and Eel* · black and white chalk on green-gray paper, 305 x 108 mm. (12 x 16¼")
New York, Cooper Union

Plate 41
François BOUCHER · *A Cottage by a Lake* · black chalk on gray paper, 260 x 376 mm. (10¼ x 14¾") · Paris, Jean Cailleux

Plate 42

Claude GILLOT · *Voltaire receiving Alexis Piron* · sanguine, gray wash, pink water color and touches of black ink, 130 x 174 mm. (5⅛ x 6⅞") · New York, Harry G. Sperling Collection

Plate 43
Jean Antoine WATTEAU
*Young Girl Bending Over*
black and red chalk on warm or
pinkish tan paper, 260 x 136 mm.
Frankfort on Main
Staedel Art Institute

Plate 44

François BOUCHER · *Boy Fishing* · black and white chalk on blue paper, 300 x 443 mm. (11⅞ x 17½")
Art Institute of Chicago · Joseph and Helen Regenstein Collection

Plate 45

François BOUCHER • *Landscape with Rustic Bridge* • black chalk, heightened with white, on buff paper, 203 x 280 mm. (8 x 11")
New York, Mr. and Mrs. Charles Slatkin

Plate 47
Jean Antoine WATTEAU · *Five Studies of a Dromedary* · red and black chalk, 305 x 426 mm. (12 x 16¾")
New York, Mr. and Mrs. Charles Slatkin

Plate 46
Jean Antoine WATTEAU
*Nude on Sofa*
red and black chalk on
light-bluish-gray paper
225 x 254 mm. (8⅞ x 10")
London, The British Museum

79

Plate 48

François BOUCHER
*Venus with the Target*
crayon and pastel on paper
438 x 307 mm. (17¼ x 12¼₁₆")
St. Louis, City Art Museum

Plate 49

François BOUCHER • *Study of a Rooster* • black, red and white chalk on sand-colored paper, 190 x 200 mm. (7½ x 7⅞")
Stockholm, Nationalmuseum

82

Plate 50
Louis TOCQUÉ
*Portrait of Marie-Thérèse Lemoyne*
black chalk on tan paper
295 x 248 mm. (11½ x 9⅝")
New York
Mr. and Mrs. Benjamin Sonnenberg

Plate 51
Hubert-François Bourguignon
called GRAVELOT
*Portrait Sketch of a Man*
red chalk, 273 x 194 mm.
(10¾ x 7⅝")
New York, Cooper Union

Plate 52
Maurice-Quentin de LA TOUR
*Portrait of M. Louis de Silvestre*
black and white chalk on green
paper with touches of red
and blue, 300 x 250 mm.
(11¾ x 9⅞")
Art Institute of Chicago
Joseph and Helen Regenstein
Collection

Plate 53
Maurice-Quentin
de LA TOUR
*Self-Portrait*
pastel with touches of black
crayon on buff paper
270 x 170 mm. (10⅝ x 6¾")
Paris, Louvre

Plate 54
François BOUCHER
*Valet with a Coffee Pot*
red, black and white chalk and
graphite, 345 x 195 mm.
(13⅝ x 7⅝")
Joseph and Helen Regenstein
Collection
Art Institute of Chicago

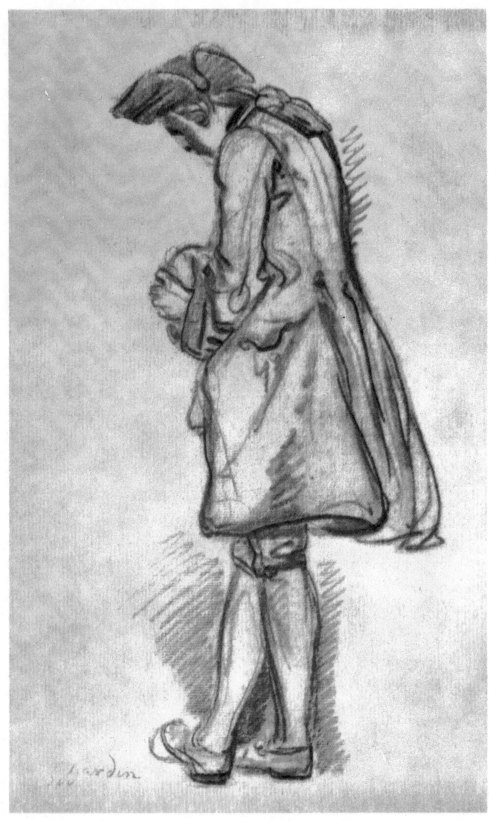

Plate 55
Jean-Baptiste Siméon CHARDIN
(attributed to)
*Young Man Holding a Bowling Ball*
sanguine on white paper
347 x 225 mm. (13 $^{11}\!/_{16}$ x 8 $^{7}\!/_{8}$")
Paris, Louvre

Plate 56
Gabriel de ST. AUBIN
*Portrait of a Clockmaker*
black chalk and water color
heightened with gouache
232 x 150 mm. (9⅛ x 5¹⁵⁄₁₆")
Newport, Rhode Island
Forsyth Wickes

Plate 57
Louis Carrogis
de CARMONTELLE
*Countess Cossée*
black and red chalk and water
color, 310 x 200 mm. (12¼ x 7⅞")
Art Institute of Chicago
Gift of Robert Allerton

Plate 58
François BOUCHER
*Seated Nude*
red, black and white chalk on tan
paper, 371 x 235 mm. (14⅝ x 9¼")
Washington, D.C.
Mrs. Hubert Chanler

Plate 59
François BOUCHER · *The Three Graces* · black and white chalk on brownish paper, 260 x 343 mm. (10¼ x 13½")
Bradford, Pennsylvania, T. Edward Hanley

Plate 60

Gabriel de ST. AUBIN • *Players (Irruption de Chanteurs Costumes)* • pen and ink with water color and gouache on tan paper
203 x 260 mm. (8 x 10¼") • New York, Mrs. Herbert N. Straus

Plate 61
Augustin de St. AUBIN
*Chevalier of Liroux*
*Playing the Bassoon*
lead pencil on white paper
195 x 138 mm. (7¹¹⁄₁₆ x 5⁷⁄₁₆")
Cologne
Wallraf-Richartz Museum

Plate 63
Pierre-Jean BOCQUET
*Demonio, Senor Remon*
*Costume* for an Opera
pen and bistre wash with
some red wash on white
paper, 302 x 235 mm.
(11⅞ x 9¼")
Rhode Island
Private Collection

Plate 64

Jean-Baptiste PILLEMENT · *Chinoiserie Fantasy* · pencil, 222 x 292 mm. (8¾ x 11½") · New York, Cooper Union

**Plate 65**
Louis-Philibert DEBUCOURT · *The Dressing Room of the Extras of the Comédie Française* · gray and black wash over black chalk, 333 x 447 mm. (13⅛ x 17⅝") · Art Institute of Chicago, Joseph and Helen Regenstein Collection

Plate 66
Jacques André PORTAIL
*Portrait of Monsieur
and Madame Fredou*
pencil and sanguine
343 x 280 mm. (13½ x 11")
Cambridge, Massachusetts
Harvard University
Courtesy of the
Fogg Art Museum

Plate 67
Jean-Baptiste GREUZE
*Head of a Girl*
red chalk, 417 x 302 mm.
(16 x 11⅞")
Worcester Collection

Plate 68
Jacques-Louis DAVID
*Princess Murat and*
*Pauline Borghese*
pencil on white paper, squared
236 x 178 mm. (9⅜ x 7")
Cambridge, Massachusetts
Harvard University
Courtesy of the
Fogg Art Museum

Plate 69
Jacques-Louis DAVID
*Study for "The Oath of*
*the Tennis Court"*
pencil and pen wash
390 x 255 mm. (15½ x 10")
Art Institute of Chicago
Joseph and Helen Regenstein
Collection

Plate 71
Jean-Baptiste GREUZE • *The Return of the Prodigal Son* • pen and wash over black chalk, 370 x 505 mm. (14⅝ x 20″)
Art Institute of Chicago, Gift of Mr. and Mrs. Leigh B. Block

Plate 70
Jean-Honoré FRAGONARD • *The Sultan*
brush and bistre wash on white paper
374 x 277 mm. (15¼ x 10⅞″)
New York, Mr. and Mrs. Walter C. Baker

Plate 73

Pierre-Paul PRUD'HON • *Minerva, Poet Laureate and Other Studies* (verso: *Embracing Genii*) • Chinese white and brown wash over graphite on blue paper, 290 x 442 mm. (11⅜ x 17⅜")

Art Institute of Chicago, Print and Drawing Department, Purchase Fund

Plate 72

Pierre-Paul PRUD'HON

*Head of Vengeance*

Study for *Justice and Vengeance*

*Pursuing Crime* (1808) • black and white

chalk and estompe on blue paper

510 x 395 mm. (20 x 15½")

Art Institute of Chicago

The Arthur Heun Fund

Plate 74
Jean-Honoré FRAGONARD
*Odorico Kills Corebo*
black chalk and brush with bistre
wash, 388 x 241 mm. (15¼ x 9½")
Washington, D.C.
Phillips Memorial Gallery

Plate 75
Jean-Honoré FRAGONARD
*Portrait of Benjamin Franklin*
wash, 278 x 238 mm. (10⅞ x 9⅜")
Art Institute of Chicago
Given in Memory of
Charles Netcher II

Plate 76
Pierre-Paul PRUD'HON · *The Cruel One Laughs at the Tears He Has Caused to be Shed (Cupid Laughing at Love)*
black and white chalk on blue paper, traced for transfer, 236 x 317 mm. (9⅝ x 12½") · New York, Pierpont Morgan Library

Plate 77
Théodore GÉRICAULT
*Mounted Officer of the Carabineers*
*(Seen from the Back)*
black chalk with water color, heightened
with white, 254 x 215 mm. (10 x 8½")
Paris, Louvre

Jean-Honoré FRAGONARD · *Bull in a Stable* (Taureau de la Campagne Romaine) · bistre wash, 350 x 490 mm. (13¾ x 19⁵⁄₁₆″)
New York, Georges Wildenstein

**Plate 79**
Hubert ROBERT · *An Italian Garden Scene* · red chalk on off-white paper, 218 x 310 mm. (8⁹⁄₁₆ x 12³⁄₁₆″) · The Clowes Fund Inc.

Plate 80

François-Marius GRANET · *Entrance to the Park of Versailles on the Orangerie Side* · water color, 220 x 354 mm. (8⅝ x 14")
Paris, Louvre

Plate 81
Jean Auguste
Dominique INGRES
*Portrait of
M.F.C.H.L. Pouqueville*
pencil on white paper
305 x 230 mm. (12 x 9¼16")
New York, David Daniels

Plate 82

Hubert ROBERT • *Round Fountain in a Roman Garden* • red chalk, 307 x 435 mm. (12⅛ x 17⅛")
Art Institute of Chicago • Gift of Tiffany and Margaret Blake

Plate 83
Hubert ROBERT
*Imaginary Roman Landscape*
pen, sanguine, bistre wash, 362 x 285 mm.
(14¼ x 11¼") • Paris, Jean Cailleux

114

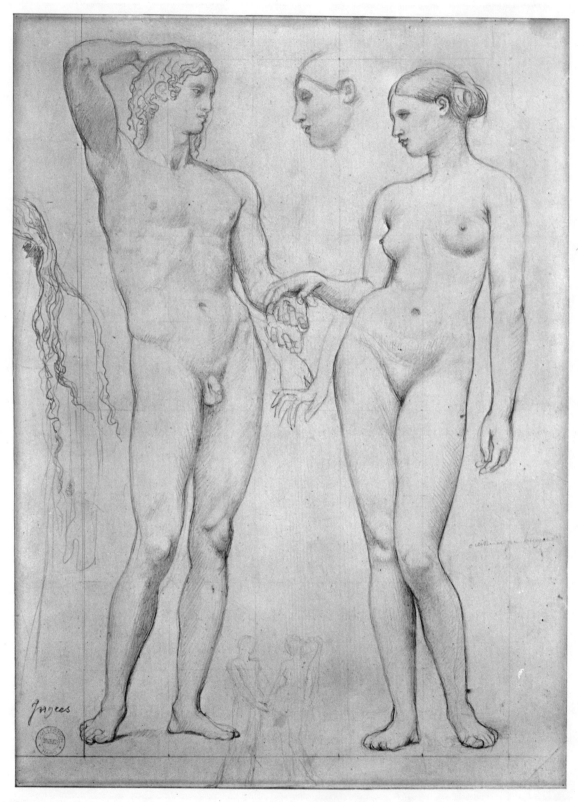

Plate 84
Jean Auguste
Dominique INGRES
*Two Nudes*, Study for
"*The Golden Age*"
pencil on white paper
faded to ivory, outlined with
a stylus, 390 x 281 mm.
(15⅜ x 11¹⁄₁₆")
Cambridge, Massachusetts
Harvard University
Courtesy of the
Fogg Art Museum,
Bequest of
Grenville L. Winthrop

Plate 85
Jean Auguste
Dominique INGRES
*A Study of Three Men
on Horseback*
black crayon on white
paper, 544 x 413 mm.
(21⁷⁄₁₆ x 16¼")
Kansas City, Missouri
Nelson Gallery of Art

Plate 86
Hubert ROBERT
*Arch of Titus in Rome at Night*
sanguine on yellowed paper
508 x 357 mm. (24 x 14⅟₁₆")
Cologne
Wallraf-Richartz Museum

Plate 87
Jean Michel MOREAU
*The Disclosure of Pregnancy*
pen and brown wash
270 x 220 mm. (10⅝ x 8¹¹⁄₁₆")
Detroit, Michigan
Mrs. Henry Ford II

Plate 88
Jean Auguste
Dominique INGRES
*Female Nude*
pencil on white paper
278 x 296 mm. (10¹⁵⁄₁₆ x 11⅝")
Bayonne, Musée Bonnat

Plate 89

Jean Auguste
Dominique INGRES
*Young Man*
pencil, 290 x 220 mm.
(11 7/16 x 8 11/16″)
Rotterdam
Museum Boymans-
van Beuningen

Plate 90

Anne-Louis GIRODET · *Judgment of Midas* (recto) · black crayon, pen, bistre wash and India ink wash with highlights of white gouache on two sheets of paper pasted together at the center, 302 x 500 mm. (11⅞ x 19¾") · Paris, Louvre

Plate 91
Jacques-Louis DAVID
*Standing Man in a Pose
of Proclamation*
pen and ink on tan paper
378 x 248 mm. (14⅞ x 9¾")
New York
Mr. and Mrs. Walter C. Baker

Plate 92
Théodore CHASSÉRIAU
*Portrait of Madame Borg
de Balsam*
pencil on white paper
340 x 270 mm. (13⅜ x 10⅝")
Philadelphia, Pennsylvania
Mr. Henry P. McIlhenny

Plate 93
Jean Auguste
Dominique INGRES
*Study for the Portrait
of Madame Moitessier*
pencil, 305 x 235 mm.
(12 x 9¼") · New York
Georges Wildenstein

Plate 95
Théodore GÉRICAULT · *Mars and Hercules* · pen and ink over black chalk on white paper, 200 x 270 mm. (7⅞ x 10⅝")
Lille, Palais des Beaux-Arts, Musée Wicar

Plate 94
Pierre-Paul PRUD'HON
*Count of Sommariva* (detail)
black crayon, heightened with white,
on blue-gray paper, 171 x 245 mm.
(6¾ x 9⅝") · New York
Mr. and Mrs. Benjamin Sonnenberg

127

Plate 96

Constantin GUYS · *Carriage and Three Gentlemen on Horseback* · pen and water color, 159 x 260 mm. (6¼ x 10¼")
New York, Cooper Union

# Biographies

**BELLANGE**, Jacques
Jacques Bellange (ca. 1575-ca. 1638) was a portraitist and decorative painter in the service of Duke Charles III of Lorraine from 1600-1617. He combined Italian Mannerism with northern Gothic traditions.

**BERAIN**, Jean
Jean Berain (1638-1711) was an engraver, draughtsman and designer of ornaments for the decorative arts.

**BOCQUET**, Pierre-Jean
Pierre-Jean Bocquet or Boquet (1751-1817) was a landscape painter and engraver whose best-known works were on the theme of mountain forests showing wild animals. He also worked from 1809-'10 on designs at the Sèvres porcelain factory.

**BOUCHER**, François
François Boucher (1703-1770), the principal painter to Louis XV and drawing master to Madame Pompadour, was also an illustrator, decorator, engraver and chief designer for Beauvais tapestries.

**BOULLE**, André Charles
André Charles Boulle (1642-1732) was the first to serve as Cabinet-Maker to Louis XIV, making magnificent furniture inlaid with bronze, copper, and tortoise shell based on his own designs and those of Charles LeBrun. He supervised a large studio in which his sons worked.

### CALLOT, Jacques

Jacques Callot (1592-1635), an engraver, went to Rome and Florence where he learned etching. Courtiers, actors of the *commedia dell'arte,* gypsies and beggars formed his chief subject matter until after the death of his patron, Cosimo II, and his return to France, when he represented the horrors and grotesqueries of war.

### CARMONTELLE, Louis Carrogis de

Louis Carrogis de Carmontelle (1717-1806) was a French portrait painter who painted the most eminent people of his day, mostly in profile.

### CHARDIN, Jean-Baptiste Simeon

Jean-Baptiste Simeon Chardin (1699-1779) was a member of the Academy and served as its treasurer and as arranger of paintings in the Louvre. His street scenes, courtyard interiors, still life and domestic genre scenes were based on direct observation.

### CHASSÉRIAU, Théodore

Théodore Chasseriau (1819-1865) was born in Santo Domingo. He became a pupil of Ingres at the age of ten. Later he abandoned the academic style and became an admirer of Delacroix's work. He was the forerunner of Gustave Moreau and Puvis de Chavannes.

### CLAUDE Lorrain

Claude Gellée, known as Claude Lorrain (1600-1682), was a great landscape painter, the first to study natural lighting effects and thus became the forerunner of Corot, Turner and the Impressionists of the 19th century. In Italy he was a pupil of Agostino Tassi and Paul Brill and was influenced by Poussin.

## CLOUET, François

François Clouet (ca. 1522-1572) was a pupil of his father, Jean, from whom he inherited the title "Painter to the King." His portraits were greatly appreciated in his own time although few of the works ascribed to him can now be authenticated.

## CLOUET, Jean

Jean Clouet (ca. 1475-1541) was a painter—probably of Flemish origin. Few works can be definitely attributed to him and little is known about his life except that he was a court painter to Louis XII and François I and lived most of his life in Tours.

## DAVID, Jacques Louis

Jacques Louis David (1748-1825) studied with historical painter Josef Marie Vien and won the Prix de Rome in 1774. He was first influenced by Boucher, and, when working in Rome, by the classic revival. Politically active during the Revolution, he later became first painter to Napoleon. He had widespread influence as leader of the neoclassic movement, although today it is his portraits that are most highly regarded.

## DEBUCOURT, Louis-Philibert

Louis-Philibert Debucourt (1775-1832) was a painter and engraver who first studied historical painting under Josef Marie Vien, but his chief fame lay in his treatment of genre themes or "little subjects in the Flemish-Dutch manner." He also worked with sculptors and did a series of portraits at the court of Louis XVI.

**DESHAYES, Jean-Baptiste**

Jean-Baptiste Henri Deshayes (1729-1765) was a painter of biblical and mythological themes and a designer for Gobelin and Beauvais tapestries.


**DESPORTES, Alexander**

Alexander François Desportes (1661-1743) was, along with Oudry with whom his work is often confused, one of the two great animal painters of 17th-century France.


**FOUQUET, Jean**

Jean Fouquet or Jehan Foucquet (ca. 1415/20-1480) was a miniature painter and the founder of the 15th-century school of French painting which shows influence of the van Eycks and early Florentines. He was court painter to Louis XI.


**FRAGONARD, Jean-Honoré**

Jean-Honoré Fragonard (1732-1806) studied under Chardin and Boucher and went to Rome. He especially admired the colors of the Venetian painter Tiepolo. He was the last of the great French decorative painters of the 18th century.


**GÉRICAULT, Théodore**

Jean-Louis André Théodore Géricault (1791-1824) was a pupil of Vernet and later of Guerin at whose studio he met Delacroix. He was influenced by Rubens and Michelangelo after a trip to Italy. Predominantly a painter of horses, he introduced the race-course genre (inspired largely by a trip through the English countryside) into French painting.

**GILLOT**, Claude

Claude Gillot (1673-1722) was a painter, engraver, and illustrator and the teacher of Watteau. For thirty years he was in charge of decorating and costuming the Paris Opera.

**GIRODET**, Anne-Louis

Anne-Louis Girodet de Roucy Trionson (1767-1824) was a pupil of David. He won the Prix de Rome in 1789 but drifted away from political subject matter and neoclassic treatment to more Romantic subjects, using chiaroscuro effects.

**GOURMONT**, Jean de

Jean de Gourmont (ca. 1483-ca. 1551), a painter and engraver, worked with his brothers in Paris until 1551 when he settled in Lyons, then a center of the graphic arts.

**GRANET**, François Marius

François Marius Granet (1775-1849) was an architectural and historical painter who studied with the landscape painter, Constantin, and at the atelier of David in Paris. His paintings consist chiefly of the interiors of churches and other buildings, with some historical scenes and fine portraits.

Hubert-François Bourgignon, called **GRAVELOT**

Hubert-François Bourgignon, called Gravelot (1699-1773), artist and engraver, was one of the leading illustrators in France and England during the 18th century.

**GREUZE**, Jean-Baptiste

Jean-Baptiste Greuze (1725-1805) was enormously popular in his own time as a painter of genre scenes which often pointed a moral and emphasized the homely virtues.

**GROS**, Jean-Antoine

Baron Jean-Antoine Gros (1771-1835) studied under David and became one of the official painters of Napoleon. Despite his classical training, his work had Romantic features which occasioned criticism by David. After that, his art underwent a rapid deterioration, and he became a suicide by drowning.

**GUYS**, Constantin

Constantin Guys (1805-1892) is considered a 19th-century parallel to Gabriel de St. Aubin as the chronicler of his times. He was best known for his drawings of fashions and was a war correspondent for the *Illustrated London News.*

**Master I. D. C.**

Master I. D. C. worked between 1573 and 1593 but nothing is known about his life. There are six portraits signed I. D. C. This master developed the French crayon portrait to its highest point and forecast the early 17th-century pastel-portrait mastery of Nanteuil.

**INGRES**, Jean Auguste Dominiques

Jean Auguste Dominiques Ingres (1780-1867), the painter, is considered one of the great draughtsmen of all time. A pupil of David, he also studied in the Louvre and spent many years in Rome. He epitomized the academic viewpoint in painting. His subject matter ranged from neoclassic to more Romantic exotic and oriental themes and repeatedly demonstrated his admiration for the painters of the Quattrocento and for Raphael. Today he is most admired for his masterly portraits, especially those in pencil.


## LAGNEAU, François
François Lagneau or Lanneau (ca. 1590-1666) was a draughtsman and portrait painter about whose life little is known. He was one of the first realists in French art—recording ugly subjects, drunkards and ravaged old age.


## LANCRET, Nicolas
Nicolas Lancret (1690-1743) entered the Academy as a painter of *fêtes galantes*. Unsuccessful as an historical painter, he became one of the principal imitators of Watteau and of Gillot. He also worked as an engraver.


## LA TOUR, Maurice Quentin de
Maurice Quentin de La Tour (1704-1788), a portrait painter in pastel, is considered the great pastelist of the 18th century. His portraits had an unusually lively quality, and the characterizations were strong and occasionally satiric.


## LE BRUN, Charles
Charles Le Brun (1619-1690), a pupil of his father and of Vouet, was a decorative painter who was responsible for much of the work done in Versailles. Working first for finance minister Fouquet and then Colbert, he became director of the Gobelin tapestry manufactory in 1663.

## LE NAIN, Louis

Louis Le Nain (1593-1648) is generally considered more important than his brothers, Mathieu (1588-1648) and Antoine (1607-1677), but all were famous for their scenes of peasant life.

## LE SUEUR, Eustache

Eustache Le Sueur (1616/17-1655) was a pupil of Simon Vouet and was also influenced by Raphael and Poussin. His subject matter was primarily religious and demonstrates the religious reforms apparent in the austerity of Jansenism and in the rise of Jesuit influence at that time when much of the art was secular.

## MIGNARD, Pierre

Pierre Mignard, called Mignard Le Romain (1612-1695), was called to Paris by Louis XIV as the successor to Charles Le Brun. He is best known for his court portraits.

## MOREAU, Jean Michel

Jean Michel Moreau, called Moreau the Younger, (1741-1814), was a draughtsman, illustrator of the works of Molière, Voltaire and Rousseau, and engraver who became draughtsman to Louis XVI and again, after the Restoration, to Louis XVIII. He recorded the costumes of his day in a systematic way for the *Monument du costume* as well as scenes of contemporary life.

## NANTEUIL, Robert

Robert Nanteuil (ca. 1623-1678) was a draughtsman and engraver, working in Paris, where he eventually received the title "Draughtsman to the Cabinet." His work consisted primarily of pastel portraits which he later transcribed as engravings.

### OUDRY, Jean-Baptiste

Jean-Baptiste Oudry (1686-1755) was a French painter and engraver whose early years were spent painting portraits and votive pictures for churches. Turning almost exclusively to animal and landscape painting, he became a favorite of Louis XV and was commissioned to do royal hunting scenes and to paint the king's collection of wild animals. As an illustrator, he made drawings for the *Fables* of La Fontaine.

### PILLEMENT, Jean-Baptiste

Jean-Baptiste Pillement (1727-1808) was a painter, engraver and designer who specialized in the popular *chinoiserie* subjects. His designs for manufactured silks were used in the decorative arts for upholstery fabrics, hangings and wall coverings.

### PORTAIL, Jacques-André

Jacques-André Portail (1695-1759) was an engraver and draughtsman who excelled in realistic detail. His works formed a link between Watteau and Chardin in subject matter.

### POUSSIN, Nicolas

Nicolas Poussin (1594-1665) was a landscapist and the founder of painting in the classic tradition. He studied classical sculpture in Rome and was also influenced by Titian's colors. Returning to Paris, he was court painter to Louis XIII. Since his style was not adapted to the decorative arts in demand at the time, he returned to Rome where his works became more idealized.

**PRUD'HON, Pierre Paul**

Pierre Paul Prud'hon (1758-1823) traveled in Italy and was influenced by the works of Correggio and Leonardo as evidenced in his atmospheric light and color effects. He painted portraits and historical and mythological subjects.

**RIGAUD, Hyacinth**

Hyacinth François Rigaud (1659-1743) was the principal portrait painter at the courts of Louis XIV and XV and painted most of the important people of his time.

**ROBERT, Hubert**

Hubert Robert (1733-1808) was a painter and landscape architect for Louis XVI. After the Revolution, he became Curator of the Louvre. His subjects were chiefly Roman ruins and the architecture of Paris, gardens, fountains, and staircases.

**ST. AUBIN, Augustin de**

Augustin de St. Aubin (1736-1807) was a French painter and engraver who was taught drawing by his brother, Gabriel. He made engravings after Veronese and Titian and was particularly noted for contemporary portraits.

**ST. AUBIN, Gabriel-Jacques de**

Gabriel-Jacques de Saint Aubin (1724-1780) is considered one of the greatest of the "little masters" of the 18th century and is important as one of the chief recorders of the manners and customs of his time.

## SILVESTRE, Israel

Israel Silvestre (1621-1691), a French painter and engraver who imitated Stefano della Bella and Jacques Callot, was noted for his landscapes and views which he decorated with small, precise and spirited figures. Louis XVI employed him in designing and engraving views of royal palaces and public festivals.

## TOCQUÉ, Louis

Louis Tocqué (1696-1772), born in Paris, the son of a portrait painter, studied first under Victor Bertin and later under Nattier, whose daughter he married. He painted court portraits in St. Petersburg from 1756-'58, and spent most of the following year working in Copenhagen before returning to Paris.

## VOUET, Simon

Simon Vouet (1590-1649) went to Constantinople in 1611 and visited Italy on his return, remaining until 1627. While there, he developed his theatrical compositions. He served as First Painter to Louis XIII for twenty-two years until his death.

## WATTEAU, Jean Antoine

Jean Antoine Watteau (1694-1721) studied theater design in Paris and later with the painter Gillot. He is considered today to be one of the greatest draughtsmen in history. His work was highly ornamental and graceful, free from the conventions of his time.

# Bibliography

**GENERAL**

Adhémar, J. *French Drawings of the XVIth Century,* New York, 1955.

Blunt, A. *The French Drawings...at Windsor Castle,* London, 1945.

Châtelet, A., and Thuillier, J. *Französische Malerei von Fouquet bis zu Poussin,* Geneva, 1963.

Jacques, C. (Sterling). *La Peinture française: les peintres du Moyen Age,* Paris, 1941.

Lavallée, P. *Le dessin du XIIIe au XVIe siècle,* Paris, 1930.

Lavallée, P. *Le Dessin française,* Paris, 1948.

Sterling, C. *La Peinture française, les primitifs,* Paris, 1938.

Vallery-Radot, J. *Le Dessin français du XVIIe siècle,* Lausanne, 1953.

**BELLANGE**

Pariset, F. G. *Deux Dessins de J. de Bellange,* Nancy, 1951.

**CALLOT**

Lieure, J. *Jacques Callot* (2 vols.), Paris, 1929.

**CLAUDE**

Hind, A. M. *The Drawings of Claude Lorrain,* London and New York, 1925.

Roethlisberger, M. *Claude Lorrain, The Paintings* (2 vols.), New Haven, 1961.

**CLOUET**

Moreau-Nélaton, E. *Les Clouet et leur émules* (3 vols.), Paris, 1924.

**FOUQUET**

Cox, T. *Jehan Foucquet,* London, 1931.

Perls, K. *Jean Fouquet,* London, 1940.

Wescher, P. *Jean Fouquet,* Basel, 1947.

**FRAGONARD**

Ananoff, A. *L'Oeuvre dessiné de Fragonard,* Paris, 1961.

Fosca, F. *Les Dessins de Fragonard,* Lausanne, 1954.

Mongan, E., Hofer, P., and Seznec, J. *Fragonard Drawings for Ariosto,* New York, 1945.

Reau, L. *Fragonard,* Brussels, 1956.

**GÉRICAULT**

Courthion, P. and Cailler, P. *Géricault,* Geneva, 1947.

Eitner, L. *Géricault, an Album in Chicago,* Chicago, 1960.

Gauthier, M. *Géricault,* Paris, 1935.

**INGRES**

Alazard, J. *Ingres et l'Ingrisme,* Paris, 1950.

Mathey, J. *Ingres Dessins,* Paris, n.d.

Mongan, A. *Ingres, 24 Drawings,* New York, 1947.

Naef, H. *Rome vue par Ingres,* Lausanne, 1960.

**POUSSIN**

Friedlaender, M. J. *The Drawings of Nicolas Poussin* (3 vols.), London, 1939-53.

**SAINT-AUBIN**

Dacier, E. *Gabriel de Saint-Aubin* (2 vols.), Paris, 1929-31.

**TOCQUÉ**

Doria, A. *Louis Tocqué,* Paris, 1929.

**WATTEAU**

Brinckmann, A. E. *J. A. Watteau,* Vienna, 1943.

Parker, K. T., and Mathey, J. *Antoine Watteau: Catalogue complet de son oeuvre dessiné* (2 vols.), Paris, 1957.